Pebble®

T0080599

Gran

Revised and Updated

by Lola M. Schaefer

Consulting Editor: Gail Saunders-Smith, PhD

Capstone press®

Mankato, Minnesota

Pebble Books are published by Capstone Press,
1710 Roe Crest Drive, North Mankato, Minnesota 56003.
www.capstonepub.com

Copyright © 2008 by Capstone Press, a Capstone imprint.
All rights reserved. No part of this publication may be reproduced in whole or in part, or stored in a retrieval system, or transmitted in any form or by any means, electronic, mechanical, photocopying, recording, or otherwise, without written permission of the publisher.
For information regarding permission, write to Capstone Press,
1710 Roe Crest Drive, North Mankato, Minnesota 56003.

Library of Congress Cataloging-in-Publication Data
Schaefer, Lola M., 1950–
Grandmothers/by Lola M. Schaefer. — Rev. and updated.
p. cm. — (Pebble books. Families)
Includes bibliographical references and index.
Summary: "Simple text and photographs present grandmothers and how they interact with their families" — Provided by publisher.
ISBN-13: 978-1-4296-1226-5 (hardcover)
ISBN-10: 1-4296-1226-6 (hardcover)
ISBN-13: 978-1-4296-1755-0 (softcover)
ISBN-10: 1-4296-1755-1 (softcover)
1. Grandmothers — Juvenile literature. 2. Grandmothers — Pictorial works— Juvenile literature. I. Title. II. Series.
HQ759.9.S35 2008
306.874'5 — dc22 2007027097

Note to Parents and Teachers

The Families set supports national social studies standards related to identifying family members and their roles in the family. This book describes and illustrates grandmothers. The images support early readers in understanding the text. The repetition of words and phrases helps early readers learn new words. This book also introduces early readers to subject-specific vocabulary words, which are defined in the glossary section. Early readers may need some assistance to read some words and to use the Table of Contents, Glossary, Read More, Internet Sites, and Index sections of the book.

Printed in the United States 5469

Table of Contents

Grandmothers. 5
Busy Grandmothers 9
At Play 15

Glossary 22
Read More 23
Internet Sites. 23
Index 24

Grandmothers

Grandmothers are mothers of fathers and mothers.

Grandmothers
have grandchildren.

BACK TO BASICS

Busy Grandmothers

Grandmothers are busy.
Grandma Jane works
at a library.

Grandma Lynn paints.

Grandma Nancy
bakes cakes.

T-SMASH

At Play

Grandmothers have fun.

Grandma Vera plays tennis.

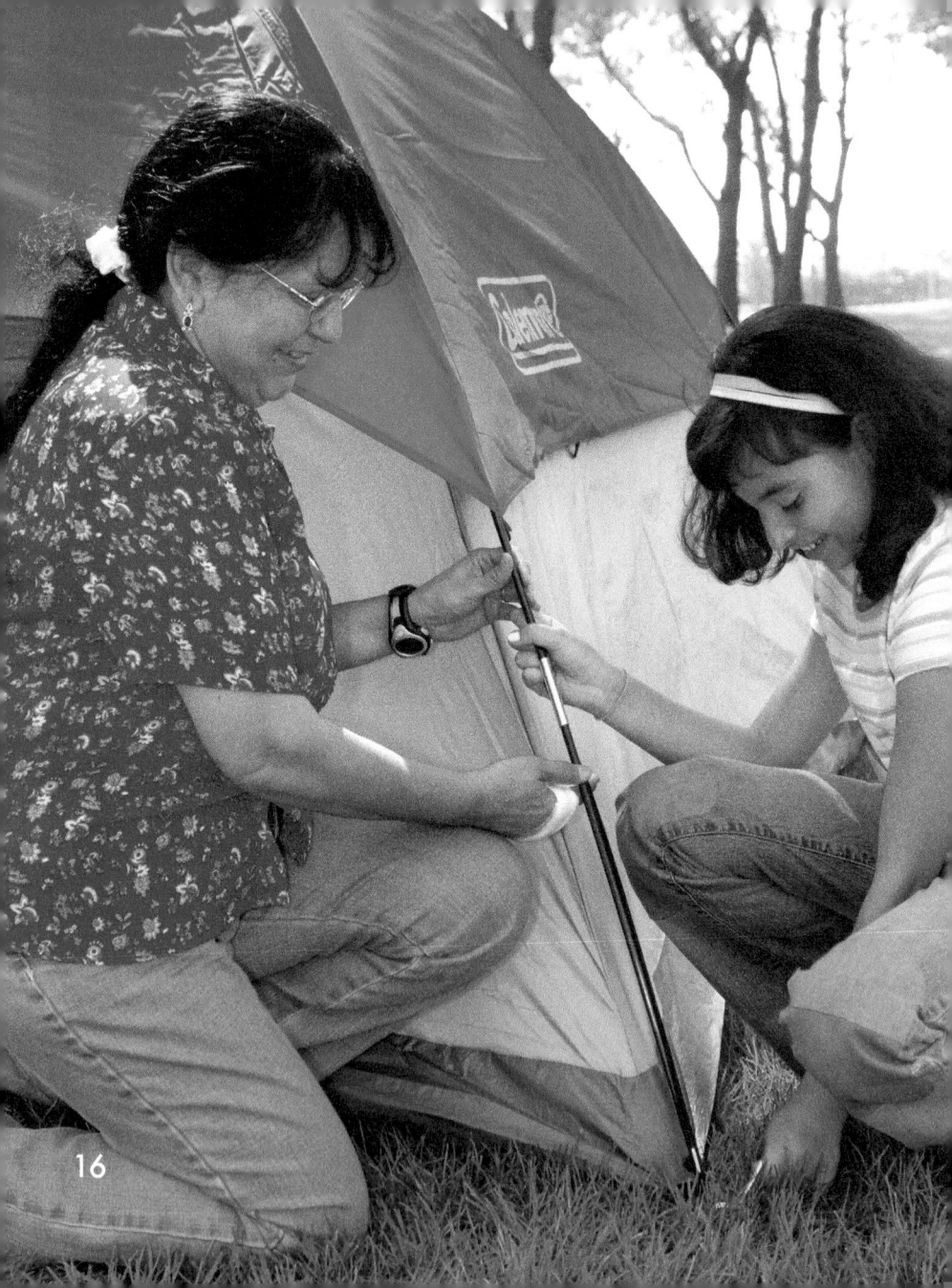

Grandma Amelia takes Paulina camping.

Grandma Martha teaches Jenny to ride a bike.

Grandmothers love
their grandchildren.

Glossary

father — a male parent; your dad's mother is your grandmother.

grandchildren — the children of a grandmother's son or daughter.

mother — a female parent; your mom's mother is your grandmother.

teach — to show someone how to do something new; grandparents often teach their grandchildren new things as they grow up.

Read More

Lord, Janet. *Here Comes Grandma!* New York: Henry Holt, 2005.

Parr, Todd. *The Grandma Book.* New York: Little, Brown, 2006.

Internet Sites

FactHound offers a safe, fun way to find Internet sites related to this book. All of the sites on FactHound have been researched by our staff.

Here's how:

1. Visit *www.facthound.com*
2. Choose your grade level.
3. Type in this book ID **1429612266** for age-appropriate sites. You may also browse subjects by clicking on letters, or by clicking on pictures and words.
4. Click on the **Fetch It** button.

FactHound will fetch the best sites for you!

Index

baking, 13
camping, 17
cousins, 7
fathers, 5
grandchildren, 7, 21
Grandma Amelia, 17
Grandma Jane, 9
Grandma Lynn, 11
Grandma Martha, 19
Grandma Nancy, 13
Grandma Vera, 15
mothers, 5
teaching, 19
working, 9

Word Count: 50
Grade 1
Early-Intervention Level: 10

Editorial Credits
Sarah L. Schuette, revised edition editor; Kim Brown, revised edition designer

Photo Credits
Capstone Press, cover; Karon Dubke, interiors